The OCTAVES

The OCTAVES

POEMS

David R. Slavitt

Louisiana State University Press

Baton Rouge

Published by Louisiana State University Press
Copyright © 2017 by David R. Slavitt
Manufactured in the United States of America
LSU Press Paperback Original
First printing

Designer: Barbara Neely Bourgoyne
Typeface: Sentinel
Printer and binder: LSI

Library of Congress Cataloging-in-Publication Data
Names: Slavitt, David R., 1935–, author.
Title: The octaves : poems / David R. Slavitt.
Description: Baton Rouge : Louisiana State University Press, [2017]
Identifiers: LCCN 2017005125| ISBN 978-0-8071-6637-6 (pbk. : alk. paper) |
   ISBN 978-0-8071-6638-3 (pdf) | ISBN 978-0-8071-6639-0 (epub) |
   ISBN 978-0-8071-6640-6 (mobi)
Classification: LCC PS3569.L3 A6 2017 | DDC 811/.54—dc23
LC record available at https://lccn.loc.gov/2017005125

"Demitasse," "Gourds," "Hafiz" "Medlar," and "Zamboanga" appeared in *Per
Contra,* #32, Summer 2014. The author thanks the editors.

The paper in this book meets the guidelines for permanence and durability of
the Committee on Production Guidelines for Book Longevity of the Council on
Library Resources. ♾

For Deborah, in memoriam.

The Lord has sworn
and will not change his mind:
"You are a priest forever,
in the order of Melchizedek."

CONTENTS

TO THE READER

The poems are easy enough; what's hard to imagine
is you, the reader, slightly smarter than I am,
but generous too: you make allowances for
the many defects you find. You've read the books,

seen the paintings, heard the music, and know
whatever I may allude to. More important,
you laugh at what amuses me, too. Your only
defect is that I cannot believe you are real.

the OCTAVES

∞

Ice skaters can do it and horses, I think,
in which event the numerical meaning blurs
and drifts off into the ether. A lemniscate?
Or a lissajous or a Bowditch curve perhaps,

describing complex harmonic motion? No,
but it could be a two-petaled rose, or an analemma...
It tires me out, as it does the figure also,
which lies down to rest in infinity.

ACCOMPANIST

So Rome is burning, and Nero is playing music,
not on a fiddle maybe, but that doesn't matter.
What's strange is that nobody mentions the poor slave
he has doing the back-up. He is the one

who understands, as the emperor does not,
how crazy this is but, not feeling free to comment,
performs as he must and even begins to enjoy it,
the fire, the screams, Nero, and playing along.

AMANITAS AND OTHERS

The old wives' tale about cooking doubtful mushrooms
and stirring them with a silver spoon to see
if the spoon turns black, as it will with the poisonous ones,
is not true. I never gather mushrooms

but I wonder, still, what mischievous old wife
invented the crazy story and passed it on
to gullible neighbors whom she must have hated
or fools she thought the world would be better without?

AMBER ROOM

Break your brain on this: in Catherine's palace
is a whole room with walls covered in amber.
Ridiculous, of course, and crazy expensive.
Germans bombed it to bits in the war. Okay?

But Putin restored it at even greater expense
to show the world how bad the Romanovs were—
no longer extravagance but criticism.
The question is, did that make it better or worse?

ANGEL

He, too, must show up when the angels assemble
in conclave in their splendid raiment. But he
dresses down and stands apart, his eyes
downcast, the angel in charge of suicides.

He does not attempt to comfort them: he knows
it can't help, for they have gone beyond that,
but he does what he can, which is to apologize
to each of them for a world that should have been better.

APOPHENIA

The welkin's welter, a sky full of random dots ...
Random, I say, even if any fool
can draw a line from any one of them
to any other. Because we cannot bear

meaninglessness, we find, or declare, meaning,
connect, see cause and effect, synergies, sense.
We know better but still persuade ourselves
so we can stand, breathe, and not despair.

BASSOON

Name me, for a hundred thousand zlotys,
one bassoonist. Anonymous and knowing
how they all deserve better, they play
dutifully and well. Oh, you've got one?

Illinois Jacquet? Was a jazz musician,
a saxophonist mostly. Another? No?
They learn humility but sometimes have
a solo in which, for a few bars, they shine.

BELL

If you send to know for whom the damned bell
tolls, the odds are that it tolls for the
newly deceased person. Or perhaps
it's just noon. Or there is a fire somewhere.

Smaller, higher bells are more interesting,
warning that a leper is coming this way
or the Good Humor man. More often than not, disaster
creeps up in the silence we've learned to fear.

BEREISHIS

Philosophers fret that something cannot come
from nothing, and they have logic on their side,
the laws of which even God must obey,
but they put the question wrong: better to ask

if God could allow the nothingness to die.
It still is a mystery but understanding
how these things work, who would feel
fear, helplessness, and the need to pray?

BLESS YOU

A sudden tickle that starts in the nose but soon
spreads to the chest to engulf the entire body,
and then the spasm comes. If we'd never sneezed,
this would be terrifying as it takes us

and stops for an instant all the body's business.
Then we return to life. Having learned?
That sneezing will not kill you. But something will,
and, if you are lucky, will feel like this.

BROTHERS

The proverb says that when your son grows up
you should make him a brother, which sounds cozy enough,
except for Cain and Abel, Esau and Jacob,
Polynices and Eteocles ... The silly

ditty Schiller wrote (*Alle Menschen*
werden Brüder) and Beethoven set to music
offers a splendid prospect, but do not hold
your breath unless you're willing to do so forever.

C^2

You approach that dizzy speed, which is, of course,
34.57 million miles
per second: physicists say that time will slow down.
When you reach that speed does it follow that time stops?

Or faster than the speed of light? What's that
but the speed of darkness, instantly everywhere,
in which we might go back to undo and unsay
the grievous errors we made in the light?

CARDS

For poker or blackjack, you want a new deck,
innocence descending yet once more
into our maculate world; but fortune tellers'
cards are limp, having been handled before

by so many or, say, by their hopes and fears
the cardboard has absorbed. Their stylized faces
are careworn as they should be. Who would consult
wisdom that wasn't painfully won over years?

CAT LOOKING AT SPIDER

The detail shows the crouching cat as it stares
At a spider in the lower left-hand corner
That we cannot see, although we may focus upon
That space outside the frame on which its body

Is fixed. Ôide Tôkô's whole painting
Gives us the spider—which is just a distraction.
The subject is that beautiful frozen patience
of the cat watching for movement. Look at that.

CHIMAERA

These fearsome chimaeras Nebuchadnezzar put up
on the blue gate would be difficult to tame
and hard no doubt to housebreak—but could there have been
miniatures, like poodles or schnauzers, friendly

albeit high-strung. The curved scorpion tail
is mostly for show as are the eagle talons,
but the scales on the body are gorgeous and that rapt
gaze of the eyes of the serpent can be endearing.

CLAUDEL

Auden took it out, for whatever reason,
but it's one of his best-known lines—about how Time
will pardon Paul Claudel for writing well.
Is Time such a fanatic litterateur?

However much he collaborated or how
much of an anti-Semite he was, he's dead,
so I can overlook it if not quite pardon.
I read him as I read Pound—to annoy him.

COMFORT

Happiness looks to the future, pride to the past.
What we have in the present is mere comfort,
but not merely mere, as Buddhists believe,
who dismiss everything else and live—or try to—

in the present as cats can. Misery, too,
and shame are elsewhere. Now there is only warm
and dry and well-fed or their opposites we
have managed to bear before and can again.

COMMUNICATION

With dictionaries, grammars, and all those aids
to understanding, I am no better off
in any language, including, I am afraid,
English, which I'm still learning. And forgetting.

Even my own idiolect. And yours.
You speak a simple sentence and I guess,
as I might with a newspaper in Portuguese,
what you might mean—and then what that might mean.

CONDOLENCE

Your last words need not be another prayer
to the bored Lord. Instead, look up from your bed
at the faces—sad, worried, or maybe impatient—
and condole with them. Let your exit line

establish you as the first of your own mourners
when, with your last breath, you contrive to join them,
saying the customary words: "May God
comfort you among all the mourners of Zion."

COUGAR

Among the big cats, only the cougar
doesn't roar. A deficiency? Perhaps,
but it is the only big cat that purrs,
and if, sometime eons ago, it chose

this over that, who would criticize?
It's still a carnivore, a predator,
but reveling in the sound of felicity,
it shows what's difficult not to think of as grace.

CURRICULUM

Master the rudiments because you will need them,
some of them anyway. But go on from there
to competence and further than that to realize
where all this diligence always gets you:

pride in yourself that you have to hide, annoyance
in the face of ignorance and tastelessness
that are everywhere, and increasing loneliness,
which is your only reliable recompense.

DANSEUSE

Oh that this tutu's solid flesh would melt,
thaw, and so forth and so on. It's a complaint
most ballerinas make during careers
that are, for the most part, painful and painfully brief.

Anorexia, shin splints, heartbreak,
and everything in between for beauty's sake?
The theater of cruelty or a bad joke we learn
to ignore—as all those in the corps have done.

DEATH CERTIFICATE

To declare your death to the rest of the world is easy—
even if the insurance adjusters, the cops,
your wife, and the IRS are after you.
The trick is sincerity: if you believe it

and can walk away from whatever your life was
until that moment, it is accomplished, whatever
the consequences may be. Why would you care?
What can they do to you or to your corpse?

DECISIONS

Choices, even the simple ones between
artichokes and leeks, may leave your hand
hovering between them, awaiting a signal
not from your mind so much as your mind's mind,

the Pythia's response to the rising vapors
that guided her inspired guesses. This or that
may not mean much or can shape the rest of your life
by what you think you have decided. Leeks.

DEMITASSE SPOON

In an up-market jumble shop in a glass case
were maybe a hundred silver spoons, all orphans,
most of them teaspoons, but some, the small
demitasse size—fallen on hard times.

The last survivors of what must have been sets
of four or six, they sprawled there, noble metal,
indifferent to death, financial ruin, theft,
and all such other vulgar vicissitudes.

DOPPLER EFFECT

Inattentive, I missed that critical moment
when everything went down by a half tone
and it was clear that what had been approaching
was speeding away, dwindling, disappearing.

Novels and poems I can reread, but some
paintings I cannot revisit. And all the great meals.
But the losses I grieve for most are the voices and faces
and even the bodies of those I once loved.

DROP

Avoiding the mops, the sinks, the toilet bowls,
and the sewers, the fortunate drop of water falls
from its cloud back to the sea from which it arose.
But how is it welcomed? What has it achieved?

The mission was to clean, to purify,
to redeem the soiled world from its inherent,
repetitive foulness, to immerse itself
and only then ascend, cleansed of its cleansing.

EXPRESS

Longeurs are shorter these days or else our speed
has increased. Back when we were children, time
never flew like this. We hurtle through it
and miss details of course. Names fade

and faces at which we peer through a smeary window
not to enjoy the scenery but trying
to guess where we are. We could not make out
that last station sign or the one before it.

FAMILY PARTY

To protect myself, I'll imagine myself encased
in a glass booth so they can see and hear me
but cannot do me bodily harm—as I
will be less of a menace to them. I can mute

my hearing aid at moments of stress and maintain
a plausibly benign expression throughout
the long evening. It may be a trial
but I shall be secure in my booth, like Eichmann.

FORTRESS

In every cell in the Peter and Paul fortress
is a window that lets the prisoner see sky
to know what he's missing—but not in the punishment cell
to which the other cells aspire, the point

of prison being punishment. Its blackness
shows the inmate that what he is deprived of
is everything. He tries to peer into the dark
and sees, in its enormity, his future.

FUGUE STATE

A fugue state should not be a dire condition,
but it isn't Bach or Handel the doctors mean,
unless they hear those relentless cascades
of notes as manifestations of derangement.

Abnormal, surely, but that merely means different
from the random noises around us. Order and beauty
rarely make their appearances in clinics
except by their lack and the patients' grim longing.

GARDENS

Going for long walks is satisfying
to those who are hunter-gatherers at heart
or adventurers whose dreams are of elsewhere.
Those who tend gardens are otherwise

disposed and believe in here, a little patch
retrieved for only a moment from the wildness
beyond the wall that cannot stand against
the looming threats from the woods and mountainsides.

GIFT

How to put self-consciousness by? To think
concedes defeat. The idea is not to have
any idea at all, to know how to shrug
all knowing off your burdened shoulders

both as actor and spectator. It must
happen of itself, as sleep can happen,
or used to, when you were young and had the gift
of having the gift—which you can barely remember.

GORMLESS TWIT

They used to soar and wheel over English gardens
in impressive profusion, and yet they were reclusive,
shy birds. The male was just as dull
in plumage as the female. One seldom found

the nests they made in the branches of dead trees.
It is said they may be related to the booby
and perhaps the dodo, although these may have sprung up
independently in several places at once.

GOURDS

They're too pretty to eat or too weird looking,
but people buy them for table decorations,
so farmers grow them. What special niche is this
for evolution to have ventured into?

Dipper gourds, snake or finger gourds...
an array of tasteless uselessness in a vital
variety, as if a gourd god with nothing
else to do were devising diverting whimsies.

HAFEZ

Hafez is a name you have to earn
by memorizing the Qur'an, every word.
But what honorific shall we award
one who has memorized the entire Torah?

What title of respect for the *Iliad,*
the *Commedia* or *Paradise Lost?* Do we want
to broadcast such information? Better not,
so that any stranger might turn out to be wise.

HERMITAGE CATS

In the Hermitage cellars and sub-cellars they say
there are fifty or sixty cats, semi-feral,
that protect the place from vermin from the Neva.
Every now and then, to reduce the clowder,

caretakers capture a few to put up for adoption
by people eager to have them—for they are the last
surviving household servants of Nikolai,
of whom the Russians are still furtively fond.

HERO

The heroic poet is said to have written in prison
poems of eloquent protest on toilet paper
in minuscule script. None of them survives,
for he understood what most poets never learn—

verse may be important but cleanliness, too,
has its worth in the world. He memorized
the poems and used the paper to wipe his ass.
If he died, they'd be lost, along with his lost pretensions.

IN THE BEGINNING

Sorry to contradict, but it wasn't a word
or a thing some word might represent, but a number,
no particular number but the rules
of numbers: how they progress, addition, subtraction,

and all the rest, waiting to be discovered
by six-year-olds now but first by God
who couldn't create a thing unless he acknowledged
what two and two were and always will be.

IN THE GAZEBO

In the late afternoon sun, the garden changes
mood as ever-lengthening shadows predict
a darkening soon to come. The light is tinged
with gold that we must neither try to hold on to

nor hasten to spend—as with an inheritance.
Summer has cooled to this equipoise, ideal
but fleeting. Sit still now and enjoy
what we long awaited and waited for us.

IPHIGENIA

How could a god ask that of Abraham,
even if he was only kidding? Still,
the idea was horrid enough to launch
a religion. And King Agamemnon did it,

killed Iphigenia: the Greeks were impressed
but not surprised, knowing that this is what happens
everywhere and all the time. Believe
that religion, if you are tough enough.

IRIS

Those purple iris surrounding the catafalque
signify royalty as well as death.
A princess then, or did the painter intend
to pay some compliment? Centuries later,

it isn't a puzzle we are required to solve,
having learned enough to see the connection,
for death, all by itself, can choose to ennoble
at least in the minds of generous, fervent mourners.

ITHAKA

On Calypso's island, what can one dream of
but waking into the world of arduous work
and small chores, the nuisances we thought
were distractions from our lives? Dry cleaning?

The dental hygienist (and new toothbrush heads)?
Milk? These are ridiculous, but the sailors,
whatever they thought they wanted, must have known
what waited for them in the Ithaka they yearned for.

JEWISH PIANO

It is meant as a slur, the incongruent name that means
"cash register," as if Jews cared
for money and nothing else. But reverse it, as one
can with any equation, and you get a grocer,

butcher, or tailor, drudging along for dollars
but also for the dream he has for his children
of music, art with its refinement, and talent
to play one day the lovely, unmodified noun.

JUDGMENT

Michelangelo had it wrong: the Judgment
doesn't take a day but only an instant.
Nobody weighs each of your good deeds
and sins on a balance. These are mere details.

It happens in a flash by which you know
who you are and what you have done, said,
and even thought. It is the first judgment
as well as the last, and nothing can be changed.

KADDISH

Her father was Jewish but never told her that.
Her mother was not Jewish, so neither was she.
Only on his deathbed does he reveal
his secret. She asks a rabbi: is it permitted

for her to recite the Kaddish for him? He laughs,
apologizes, and then asks her, "Why not?
A prayer that praises God, whom can it hurt?
Go ahead. You may even find that it helps."

KITCHEN DRAWER

From this jumble archeologists' guesses
would be all wrong, but still there was a moment
when I must have felt a need for a butter curler
and went out to buy one. Or this knife for carrots

that makes those ridges in its oval slices.
The strawberry huller I still use sometimes.
But who collected all this? Who thought his life
would be at all improved with a melon-baller?

LAST THURSDAYISM

Last Thursdayism is theism but with a joker
God recreating the world, new but the same,
every week. Why not? Making movies,
they have to put the garbage back in the streets

just as it was, to match yesterday's footage
in tribute to the present's privilege,
which none of us dares ignore. And history holds
in God's mind that he can never change.

LAUGHTER

Notice how her head goes back, her neck
stretches, her mouth opens exactly as if
this were a sexual climax—but without
the commitments, the betrayals, the taboos.

Any response in the body's sincere language
connects us intimately at least for the moment—
and often sadness follows, as when we realize
there is no hope of getting the dead to laugh.

LAUNDRY

Dick Wilbur's laundry, flapping in that alley,
may have suggested angels, or aspiration,
or a mere distaste for life in a maculate world.
It's a long line to hang such stuff on. Mine

demotes me; I become my body's servant
who can neither quit nor complain. At best, it suspends
intellect and all its pretensions: the only
thinking it requires is matching socks.

LEAVES

A gust of wind and dead leaves scurry like birds,
skimming along the grass and up in the air:
Look at them and see them inspirited,
a demonstration of energy and life.

Having been animated, at least for a moment,
movement ensues and a likeness of will—the wind's?
the leaves'? What does it matter? Eons ago
men could see miracles happen and offered prayers.

LIGHT

Before God separated light from darkness,
what was it like? A refulgent black? An opaque
glare? It is beyond imagination,
except that it isn't. What, after all, is light?

A wave but also particles, depending
on what question you're asking, and this, too,
is a contradiction that has continued since
the fourth day on which God made the sun.

LINE

The actor goes up and cannot remember the next
word, let alone line. He stands there dumb
(in both senses) and hears the prompter whisper
a phrase that doesn't prompt beyond itself.

The actor's nightmare? Or dream? Who is the author
to put words in his mouth? "The whole line please!"
he says not whispering in nonfictive words,
his own and true. And what we ought to prefer!

LION

Like the unicorn across the shield, rampant,
the lion, too, is a mythical beast but it deigns
to exist, albeit far from England. He scorns
that the earth should drink his blood and, when he is wounded,

mounts, Marlowe tells us, into the air.
It's not nonsense. Nobility of that kind,
being a marvel, prompts other marvels like it,
as Marlowe knew and, maybe, even the lions.

LOVE

Not alter when you alteration find?
What kind of madness is that? The quotidian world
has relevant information, even for lovers.
But maybe "love is not love" has another and better

meaning: the daydream subsides; the human beloved
reveals the truth of herself, which is a good thing;
and Love turns into something less and more,
unless, like Lucia or Mimi, the woman dies.

LOVE POEM

Love is not love that needs to declare itself
again and again, except perhaps as a grace note
to some other expression. Your absence evokes
only a wordless incomprehension. I manage

to dress, to eat, and to take care of this mute
creature I've become. Those ardent youngsters
who talk of desire (nothing's wrong with that)
don't know the love that waits like the cat on a pillow.

LUGGAGE

Back in the days of liners, some of the luggage
sported labels: "Not wanted on Voyage."
Who travels like that anymore? In my dreams
I keep losing suitcases, garment bags,

even trunks, full of expensive stuff.
I know, I'm getting rid of what encumbers
my life, but how else can I meet the demands
of who knows what occasions that I must face?

LYING

It's melodrama, but Violetta is still
a high-class hooker and ought to realize
that there's a way out for everyone: to swear
to Alfredo's papa whatever he wants to hear.

It's fiction of course, which is essentially lies,
and figments ought to be able to invent
further figments. "I'll never see him again"
is not so hard to say when you don't mean it.

MASS MURDER

The lunatic sprays the mall with bullets, while we
scurry along the floor for the notional cover
the planters offer and, in terror, pray,
"Don't let it be me! Please, God, not me!"

as if everyone around us except the dead
were not imploring exactly the same thing.
At last he shoots himself and we get to our feet
avoiding one another's embarrassed eyes.

MOTIONLESSNESS

A pose of motionlessness cannot conceal
the frenetic action beneath the skin of blood,
bowels, breath, &c. Outside,
the landscape dances, spinning as it whirls.

Even though you know this, you cannot believe it.
You stand stock-still, stone still, and yet your shadow
as it inches across the grass unsettles the balance
of your mind and spirit and even of your body.

MUSE

She loved me once, or said she did, perhaps
telling the truth or merely out of kindness.
Grateful, I gave her whatever I had: she seemed
pleased, but how can anyone ever tell?

She still shows up sometimes. The passion is gone
but we take tea together or have a drink.
Maybe she'll kiss my cheek in nostalgia or fondness.
Whatever it is, it's enough to keep me going.

MUSICIANS

They spend a lifetime practicing, improving,
going over the difficult passages scores
and hundreds of times. The music hangs in the air
while I'm writing. Now and then I catch a few notes.

Musicians complain about people like me, but they pose
the problem the wrong way round. Imagine rather
God looking up from his work for an instant to hear
a line or even a word or two of mine.

MUTATIONS

Among the donations to Haitian earthquake relief:
yoga mats, Frisbees, and little snap-on reindeer
antlers people put on their dogs at Christmas.
Never mind, stupid: think of the wildness, the weirdness

of such responses, or call them mental mutations,
most of them useless, on which evolution depends.
The Frisbees were maybe not such a bad idea:
even earthquake victims should have some fun.

MUTTER

The mutter is not communicative: the matter
never matters while the mind and the mouth
make their meaningless noises, the only sense
being a minimal soothing. As if, as if

something you could say could limit the damage,
improve things, or help you understand them.
But you can't, muttering can't, and your mangled speech
is the unbeliever's prayer, if he's desperate enough.

NAPS

Among the delights of second childhood, naps
rank high, that afternoon quiet time
I fought against as a boy (but what did I know?).
If sleep is the meal, these are the dainty hors d'oeuvres

that circulating angels serve the guests—
to whet their appetites? Or to help them delay
at least for a little while that banquet table,
the invitation to which we have all received?

NEANDERTAL

We wiped them out in the earth's first genocide
but not before we had interbred enough
to pick up some of their DNA, which keeps us
separate from the Africans' *sang pur.*

Call them the first Jews of eons ago
for we hated them but their genetic leaven
was what we needed to grow into what we are,
their slightly more adept, uncomfortable heirs.

NEUE SYNAGOGUE, BERLIN

"Home is home," a defiant tautology,
doesn't explain much about the Jews
who stayed on or have come back. The other
reply I got was, "We can't let them win."

Fine, but there are police outside the shul,
armed, so the issue still seems to be in doubt.
My grandfathers took a different view, less brave
but realistic, which is why I'm here and alive.

NOMAD

Nomad? No sad; no glad. They just move on
to somewhere else, free of history, free
of any particular plans for the future, while we
establish our expensive dwelling places

that turn out to be temples to terrible things
that happened there and that stained the earth forever.
Thy tabernacles are goodly, Israel,
but anything more than that defies all reason.

NOMAN

Wily Odysseus became, for the nonce, Noman—
not the one Donne says is an island,
but the man who wasn't there and yet refused
to go away. Emily's Nobody.

No mere empty category like
the present King of France, he has a sly,
shy charm only a few wraiths can claim,
and is good with children settling down for their naps.

OCTAVES

Liszt is nine: Czerny, his new teacher,
has him abandon his whole repertoire
and play nothing but exercises and scales
because, without technique, you do not exist.

You become a tyrant, a slave driver to fingers
that learn to perform faster than your brain
and take control so that you become their servant
in these exercises, running the octaves.

OMEN

Doctors can't say, and not even nurses' guesses
mean much, but cats in a nursing home
somehow know and go to lie on the beds
of dying patients on their last day. They predict,

or declare what is already present to them,
as toads can announce impending earthquakes. Egyptians,
noticing this behavior asked the cat goddess,
Bastet, to guard them and ward off evil spirits.

PANIC

Far worse has happened to me, but a sight
translation for which I am unprepared looms
in my dreams, still as I make guesses at meanings
of Latin words I should have learned: is *Odi*

Barbare, Hill's title, "Barbarian odes,"
or is it "I hate Barbarians"? Something else?
"I hate to shave," perhaps. I should have studied
longer, harder. Now I will be found out.

PASSION

Passion, the real thing, cools and either
sets or curdles. It is by nature unstable
(just as he is, just as she is), unless
some catastrophe befalls and freezes

time—and there they are, a pair of bugs
caught in a glob of amber like Héloïse
and Abelard. Dreadful, of course, but precious,
and we decorate our smug selves with their beads.

PEN

A fountain pen, if it lies on the desk too long,
will stop writing: it hasn't run out of ink
but the ink in its reservoir has dried out.
If you flush it with water you can sometimes revive it.

At the other end of the instrument, we, too,
discover that after a period of disuse
words fail us. (Ballpoint pens are immune
which is why shipping clerks and accountants like them.)

PET TIGER

Who would want one of those big cats
as a pet? It's a cruel thing to do to the tiger
or lion or puma. And dangerous, too, to the owner.
But that must be the point, to have this large

fierce thing that can turn on you any minute
at the slightest cue, or none at all. The thrill
is that of a crazy person who never knows
when he may lose it or what he then will do.

PINOCCHIO

He sang, "I've got no strings to hold me down,"
and as kids we believed him. Now we know
there are ropes of logic, hawsers of grammar, nets
of circumstance, and laws of physics from which

we try and fail to extricate ourselves.
Still, we can share at least for a moment
the puppet's silly dream of freedom that broke
Gepetto's heart and probably Collodi's.

POSTCARD

Going through boxes of papers, I find a postcard
of the Auschwitz crematorium I bought
to send someone who pissed me off, with the message:
"Warmest Regards." So far that hasn't happened.

The ugly image proclaims a copyright,
1992. (But who would infringe?)
I couldn't throw it away. I put it back
in the box in the hope that I can forget it again.

PRAYER

Nothing occurs to me? Fine. The world's
need for another poem is not pressing.
But for those who pray, and nothing happens? Their hearts
cannot perceive any response from heaven.

They can argue that, if it were always successful,
it would not be a manifestation of grace.
What faith demands is enduring the sky's indifference
without doubt. Or anger. Or chagrin.

PRESBYOPIA

The white coats think it's the lens or maybe the muscles
getting weaker, but use your eyes, man! See
how much ugliness over the years has assaulted
the retina and then, of course, the mind,

which finds whatever devices it can to dim,
blur, distance the outside's awfulness.
Turning inward, backward, it turns pages
of memory's album, hardly having to look.

RAGA

Latin, Hebrew, Sanskrit . . . The language of prayer
can be opaque and may be the better for it.
The rhythm is what counts and the modal chanting,
a dark pool of unknowing in which we float.

Intellect may fret for a bit but soon
gives up and we relax enough to regress
with the help of the sarod and the tabla's gentle
beat to an almost-forgotten infant calm.

RESTORATION

In Prešov, not far from Košice, a shul,
or say an exhibit of itself, restored,
except of course for its vanished congregation,
is open for tourists to visit and inspect.

On a wall are photographs of what it looked like
when the Nazis stabled horses in its wreck,
which is just how they should have left it, a shambles,
at least to suggest the truth of what happened here.

ROCK

A rock cannot be thirsty; it waits; it feels
nothing. (And time is almost nothing.) Rain
cannot imagine pity but it falls
and the rock's color changes, darkens, shines,

and then dries and reverts. Or so it seems
to us who have had such unpredictable moments
when we were more truly ourselves, for better or worse,
but with no better understanding than the rock.

SCOTT

Winfield—not the general but the poet—
used to go out to the study his wife had built him,
sit at the desk with the pencils all lined up,
and try to write poems, the dumb bastard.

Never try. Never sit and wait.
The muse, at moments she chooses, will interrupt
whatever you are busy with. He never
was able to figure this out: he killed himself.

SCREAMS

Like the gills we lose and the tails, there is other equipment
ontology deals out and then takes back—
those screams, for instance, from the crib or playpen
or the sandboxes and swings when they play together,

a way to attract the monkey mothers' attention
(but also the panther's?). I sit on a park bench,
my eyes closed, the warmth of the sun on my face,
and hear their cries from the universal jungle.

SECRETS

Peeling away the irrelevances the world
knows, you get down deeper to reach your secrets,
which is where the more important parts of you lurk,
wraiths among the shadows—but there you are.

You have glimpsed that fictive confidant
that would never tell a word or write a line
to betray you, but you know he may one day
desert you just before your breathing stops.

SHOWER

On my first night in Berlin in a swank hotel
I'm surprised to find neither shower curtain, nor shower.
There is a tub of course, but has the country
forsworn showers tactfully to avoid

the history they are at such pains to forget?
No, there it is, in a separate room—huge,
with aisle after aisle of showerheads and walls
of concrete still with the scratches of fingernails.

SICKBED

To lie on a sickbed, balanced on the knife-edge
of life and death is exciting. What will happen?
The physicians work on you and your body struggles
to fend off whatever they've diagnosed.

But then what? Let us say you recover
and there's no more drama. You have your life back,
but what is that? What was it? What will it be?
Now that the drama is over, you're disappointed.

SIGNS

The doctor asks how I am, but how do I know?
No symptoms, but who can say what signs
he may discover in the half-hour: Battle's
sign, Beau's lines, Beck's triad, Beevor's sign,

and hundreds more, waiting to pounce and announce
very bad things. No? Not yet? Even so,
I have to come back in four months to take my chances
again and again, until he comes up with something.

SONNETS

Octaves are fine. (What else do you think I'd say?)
But those sestets with their qualifications, revisions,
and pretension to have achieved some deeper insight?
What's with that? Why can't they wait a while

and then, when they've figured out what they want to say,
get it into the octave in the first place?
Who has the patience to keep reading on and on
until they arrive at last at the goddamned point?

SQUIRREL

Nel pino lo scoiattolo/ batte la coda a torcia sulla scorza.
　　—Eugenio Montale

The squirrel has nothing to do with the poem's business,
up in a pine tree, twitching its tail—which Montale
sees as "beating its torch like tail"—on the bark.
They do that, nervous, to keep their difficult balance

high in the tree between hunger and fear. But the vision,
the bolt of lightning, gives the little poem
life, so that, in a flash, we concede the rest,
the end of the day, the smoke, the passing cloud.

TANSY

At this late age, I learn that my birthday flower
is tansy, a kind of aster, sometimes called mugwort,
good as a cure for worms, and sometimes used
to induce abortions. It also cures flatulence.

I might have chosen a prettier plant, but it
chose me, and I must content myself
with another curious set of quirks and talents
like those that have shaped the life I thought I had made.

TEATRO OLIMPICO

An arena for dreams, its doors to left and right
allow escapes and rescues, but you are unsure
whether you're inside or out. Are those streets
or corridors? The abstract emptiness

hungers for something to happen—tragedy
or farce—that will bring life to Palladio's stark
scena, where the motes of the air dance
our lives away in a complicated frenzy.

THOREAU

Thoreau, I was taught, mowed Emerson's lawn,
a convenient arrangement by which they both disguised
an act of charity, or that's what I'd supposed
until I saw the Concord house and the lawn

the size of your dining room rug—a joke they shared.
Or was it that each believed that the other was right
living that way, writing the way he did—
or wrong and thus in need of humiliation?

THOUGHT

A thought forms, bubble bright, and pops.
What was I going to say or write? Younger,
I never worried, sure that whatever it was
would come back somehow to nag or mock. These days,

I'm less certain. A face on a train and she's gone,
along with a whole life I've just imagined
and lost forever. The world is profligate, wasteful,
a sieve through which our riches are always falling.

TOILETS

The water in the toilet is running. I jiggle
the handle. The toilet stops but the running continues
in my ear where the mind's toilet is always
flushing. The handle is missing. All night long

unless I am asleep and all day long
the toilet is going. It is a fact of nature
many old people hear: Nestor and Lear
had no toilets but heard the water running.

TOMORROW

The Guaraní may have a word that means "tomorrow,"
but they say, instead, in the Paraguayan jungle,
"if the sun rises," cautious or perhaps
unwilling to allow their gods to suppose

that they are presuming. In my tribe, too, we say
"if we live," for the same reasons. The shtetl's
superstitions turned out to be true, as we
however painfully have been forced to admit.

TOUR D'HORIZON

Tour it? You can't even get there: as you know,
horizons move whenever you do, and no
Lindblad group goes there, where what your eyes
can see gives way to speculation and dream.

There, whatever you fear or desire resides
in a landscape different for everyone who ventures
into its shimmer in which small shocking details
impress themselves on your vulnerable mind.

TWO-DOLLAR WINDOW

There aren't many left, but I can remember
how survivors used to show up at the track
at the two-dollar window to bet their tattooed numbers
in complicated combinations—trifectas,

quinellas, who knows what? Ridiculous long shots,
as if the number owed them, or as if God
who had let this happen owed them, and might repay
at least a tiny portion of what was due.

VERB

The subject verbs the object. The verb is what counts,
the word that allows motion or mere being.
God said, "Let there be..." and then the noun,
"light,"and there was light. But do not be dazzled.

Light, energy, space, and time were nothing,
still in the tohubohu until there were verbs,
older than God. The world is their handicraft,
the outcome of the dance of their conjugations.

VULTURES

A kettle of vultures comes to alight in your tree
in the backyard? The way to get rid of them
is to set off fireworks—illegal in Cambridge.
What then? You go outside and wave your arms,

utter shrill cries, or yodel maybe.
(Those are legal.) The vultures may or may not
leave, but you will feel better having found
a response, for once, to what the world has on offer.

WALLS

The first walled city, invulnerable.
With a water supply and food stored up in plenty,
they could hold out for years. As we know they did.
The Trojan War was irrelevant then, a nuisance,

but nothing for Priam to worry about. Foolproof!
Or not quite, for there are always fools
to undo the soundest plans. And Cassandra said
to leave the damned horse outside and burn it.

WOODS

Beautiful maidens turn into something else,
crones, say, with wickedness in their hearts
and souls to match their warty faces. The woods
teem with such creatures: we learned this

as children only to find out later it's true.
Stones speak, and trees; the birds say things
we might understand if we paid attention.
Look sharp; tread softly, one step at a time.

WOR

It was years ago, but I remember clearly
a woman whose fillings somehow could pick up the signal
of radio station WOR
so Long John Nebel and Jean Shepherd were always

on in her head until a dentist adjusted
the metal in her teeth and managed to stop
the modern version of that continual yammer
prophets used to hear out in the desert.

WÖRTERBUCH

is *dictionary* in German, but also in Yiddish,
a troubling language, rapidly disappearing,
so that all of its poems these days are swan songs.
I hear the Yiddish words I know in my parents'

voices. And parents, as we know, grow hazy.
English and Hebrew are thriving but arbitrary;
the soul speaks in the bits of Yiddish the *nefesh*
keeps like foreign coins in a box on the dresser.

WRITING

The poem came before there were any letters
so the bards had to memorize one line,
two, then four, and so on before going on
in their tedious craft—in which they had an advantage,

for even a dunderhead, paying attention,
would come sooner or later to see the flaws
that needed to be corrected or deleted.
That it's easier now allows us to be careless.

X

The illiterate man makes his mark with an X,
unless, a stickler, he insists upon both
family name and surname. Then, XX?
But, no, the simple X is algebraic

and can stand for any term you choose. (But how
to explain such an idea?) X marks the spot
on which he has always lived, and beyond which lurk
troubles he has never even imagined.

ZAMBOANGA

A bitter disappointment: Zamboanga
exists, can be found on maps of the Philippines,
and has deigned somehow to descend from its lofty home
shrouded in mist where it teemed with acaudate monkeys

as well as armadas of predatory whales.
But that bizarre remoteness all of us yearned for?
They harvest seaweed and pack sardines; they have
a golf club; and the rush hour traffic is bad.

ZISCA

Montaigne mentions John Zisca, a member
of Wenceslaus' court, who, wounded, ordered his skin
be flayed from his corpse and made into a drum—
to encourage his troops or bring dismay to his foes,

or possibly both. Savagery at that pitch
displays a refined calculation, mannered
enough for us to admire, for love and fear
are all but godly when boldness thus combines them.

ZWEIG

Veruchsstation für den Weltuntergang? In English,
a laboratory for the end of the world. It was,
with what we had pretended was civilization
going up in smoke that smelled of flesh.

But is this why Stefan Zweig poisoned himself?
Not exactly. Where he lived, near Rio,
there were no decent libraries, no cafés
and no relief from week after week of rain.

Lightning Source UK Ltd.
Milton Keynes UK
UKOW04f1901021017
310291UK00001B/120/P